Consulting Experts Online presents:

CEO Secrets of Non-Suck Marketing

"How To Skyrocket Your Sales & Profits By Using Proven Marketing Strategies"

Jayson Peppar

Creator/CEO,
Consulting Experts Online

Liability Disclaimer

By reading this document, you assume all risks associated with using the advice given below and within, with a full understanding that you, solely, are responsible for anything that may occur as a result of putting this information into action in any way, and regardless of your interpretation of the advice.

You further agree that our company cannot be held responsible in any way for the success or failure of your business as a result of the information presented below. It is your responsibility to conduct your own due diligence regarding the safe and successful operation of your business if you intend to apply any of our information in any way to your business operations.

Income Disclaimer

This document contains business strategies, marketing methods and other business advice that, regardless of my and my clients' own results and experience, may not produce the same results (or any results) for you. I make absolutely no guarantee, expressed or implied, that by following the advice below and within you will make any money or improve current profits, as there are several factors and variables that come into play regarding any given business.

Primarily, results will depend on the nature of the product or business model, the conditions of the marketplace, the experience of the individual, and situations and elements that are beyond your control.

As with any business endeavor, you assume all risk related to investment and money based on your own discretion and at your own potential expense.

In other words... MY RESULTS AREN'T EVEN REMOTELY TYPICAL, AND ARE IN NO WAY INTENDED TO IMPLY THAT ANYONE WILL ACHIEVE SIMILAR RESULTS, OR ANY RESULTS AT ALL FOR THAT MATTER.

WE HAVE MOST LIKELY NEVER MET. I DO NOT KNOW YOUR BUSINESS, YOUR MARGINS, YOUR MARKET, OR YOUR WORK ETHIC, THEREFORE, I WILL NOT INSULT YOUR INTELLIGENCE BY PROMISING TO "MAKE YOU RICH". ONLY YOU CAN DO THAT.

ALL BUSINESS ENTAILS RISK AND HARD WORK. DO NOT READ THIS BOOK OR APPLY FOR A CONSULTATION SESSION UNLESS YOU ARE PREPARED TO WORK HARD, STICK WITH IT, AND KEEP YOUR HEAD UP WHEN THE INEVITABLE CHALLENGES OF BUSINESS –AND LIFE– ARISE.

Consulting Experts Online presents:

CEO Secrets of Non-Suck Marketing

"How To Skyrocket Your Sales & Profits By Using Proven Marketing Strategies"

Contents

Introduction

Do you know what the most profitable skill is for running a small business? It's not managing employees. It's not having a good product, or even being the best in the world at what you do.

No. The most important skill you can have as a business owner is effectively marketing your business. Why? It doesn't matter if you're the best in the world at what you do if no one knows about your business. The only time you can bring in money is if you make sales, and you can only make sales if enough people actually know that you exist and have something to offer them.

Marketing is also the most misunderstood skill on the planet. Poor marketing is why 65% of new businesses close their doors within 24 months, and why 85% of all businesses don't even last 8 years before going under.

In this book I am going to show you the most powerful (and most profitable) marketing strategies that you can use to transform your business' bottom-line in 90 days or less.

You now have in your hands information that could positively change your business and your life... forever.

But just learning it all and having the knowledge isn't enough. You actually need to take massive action too.

Read it. Learn it. Use it. And go profit from it!

How To Get The Most Out Of Your Yellow-Page Advertising

Aside from the fact that the Yellow-Pages are now on a steep decline, both in their effectiveness and with the number of businesses purchasing adspace from them, one of the most agonizing marketing decisions a small business must make is whether to include printed Yellow-Page ads in their plan and budget. This is a big decision because:

- You commit for a full year.

- They are expensive, especially in relation to other options like paid search using Google or other Search Engine Marketing (SEM) vendors.

- You too often fail to closely track leads generated by your marketing initiatives, so when the Yellow-Page contract is up you have the same subjective decision to make all over again.

'Set-It-And-Forget-It' No Longer As Valuable

In the past, the Yellow-Pages were the only reliable resource for businesses seeking a local audience. After word-of-mouth, consumers relied heavily on the Yellow-Pages for services in a wide range of industries. And it took little work: You placed the ad, it ran for a year and you waited for the phone to ring.

Not so today. Multiple studies confirm that consumers report using the internet first (90% of the time) when they need a new product or service, and printed Yellow-Pages only second or third (less than 30% of the time.)

And even if the consumer does reach for the printed Yellow-Pages, your ad still has to stand out (size, graphics and color,) which increases the expense of being in the yellow-book. The convenience of "set it and forget it" is now trumped by the more labour intensive but more effective SEM options.

How To Measure Success

Advertising, on or offline, is not a branding exercise. It is purely about lead generation. So, with some basic math, it is not hard to understand what your own ROI is for this marketing initiative, or at the very least where your break-even point is for each campaign:

Cost of the campaign	$5,000
Value of one new customer	$100
Number of customers needed to break even	50
Number of leads needed to gain one new customer	10
Number of leads needed to break even	500
Number of leads needed to achieve 100% ROI	1000

In this case, if a Yellow-Page contract is $5,000 for the year, you need to generate 500 real leads just to break even. That is around two calls every single business day from your Yellow-Page ad, in this example. Compare this to other marketing options you have available these days, and calculate their relative break-evens.

What Should You Do At This Point?

If you think the Yellow-Pages still have value for your business, make sure.

- Immediately create a working system to track the sources of your business leads.

- Include an offer exclusively for ad respondents, with a code for them to use when calling.

- Include a dedicated phone number to make tracking easier.

- If you have a website, create a special landing-page solely for the ad (just as you would for any ad you run in any medium).

- Review your competitors' ads. What are they doing to stand out? Which competitors have dropped out in the most recent issue? If you know them, ask them why.

- Create a nice ad. For most people, 65% of the time spent looking at an ad is used to examine the image or photo, with the remaining 35% spent reading the text.

The Bottom Line

People (especially older demographics) still do reach for the printed Yellow-Pages, **when they need a local business in a hurry or emergency**.

For instance, plumbers should think hard before they ditch their local phone books. Personal injury lawyers should also track their incoming leads closely before deciding to stop their ads.

There are lots of examples of businesses that service folks with urgent needs who may benefit from staying in the yellow-books.

But, if your phone isn't ringing or your dedicated landing page is not seeing traffic from your Yellow-Page placements, stop investing in it, even if the Yellow-Pages rep is a close personal friend and a pillar down at the Chamber of Commerce. You don't run a charity, and your business needs to come first!

Have you noticed that 95% of Yellow-Page ads look the same? There's a problem with going with the "norm" – you get normal results.

With your business and livelihood on the line, I hope you're not content with average results, especially when extraordinary results are so easy to get when some basic marketing-101 is applied to your Yellow-Pages ad. You only need to do a few simple things.

The first thing you have to understand is what people are looking for when they open up the Yellow-Pages. Some people are looking for SPECIFIC contact information. They already have a service provider in mind. It's hard to get those people.

But the good news is when most people open up the yellow-book, they are looking for information to help them find the best business to contact that will give them the solution they desire.

And here's what most consumers want: They want a good deal, they want to go with someone who is able to understand their needs and lead them to the best solution, and they want to deal with as little headaches, delays and customer service problems as possible.

Now, flip open your Yellow-Pages and see if any of the ads address those points, and you'll find hardly any do so adequately.

Good! That will make it much easier for you.

I'm going to show you how to create a simple Yellow-Page ad that will make people believe that if they contact you or go into your store that they are going to get the best solution for their dollars, and it's going to be easy and convenient to deal with you, and that you're the best choice for all of their options.

If you can pull that off, you're going to get the lion's share of Yellow-Page customers in your industry.

The #1 Thing You Must Know About Yellow-Page Ads

The world's best ad is no better than the world's worst ad if no one sees it! So the first job your Yellow-Page ad must do is get the attention of the people who are best matched to take advantage of the services and products that you offer. The easiest way to do that is with a good *attention-getting headline*.

To understand what a good headline looks like, first let's look at some bad headlines. I went through my own local Yellow-Pages, and found these headlines:

"The Blind Factory" "Cyclists Serving Cyclists";

"Wet Basement or Crawl Space";

"Quality Construction"; "Professional Muffler, Inc.";

"Old Fashioned Values, Including Our Own People Doing the Work".

These are all *terrible* headlines. First, almost all of them talk about the service provider, and not the person who is looking at the ad. Talk about selfish and self-centered!

Second, none of them promise any benefit to the prospect... none of them get the person reading excited... and most are nothing more than the name of the company.

Your headline is the **most important part** of your Yellow-Page ad so you need to do much better. Ideally, you want a headline that promises a benefit to the reader, and is written to grab the attention of a certain large segment of the population who is best matched for the goods and services you provide.

Let's look at the first one: "The Blind Factory". How could this one be improved? Here is a good headline that I have found gets great results... "The 6 Mistakes Most People Make When They Purchase Blinds For Their Home...".

Or, "Warning: Don't Buy Any Blinds Until You Read This...". Or even, "How To Get The Best Blinds For Your Home In 48 Hours Or Less, Guaranteed!".

Notice the difference with these headlines? First, they focus on the consumer. Second, they promise a huge benefit. Third, they call out a certain portion of the general population – in this case, people who are looking to purchase blinds, who want to get a good deal, want ease of service, or want to make sure they don't commit a mistake when buying blinds.

Once you have a good headline, the ad practically writes itself.

For example, let's return to the headline: "The 6 Mistakes People Make When They Purchase Blinds For Their Home...".

You would then come up with 6 mistakes that you find people tend to make if they don't have an expert to help them select their product. And then, after you introduce each mistake, explain how that mistake can be avoided if they come into your store.

Remember, people who open up the Yellow-Page ads are generally looking for information to help them make the best decision on who to buy from. So typically the person who provides the most or the best information wins... and it helps if that information is all beneficial to the reader.

But if you look at the typical Yellow-Page ad, it has 50 words or less, and is usually filled with puffery, known as 'platitudes'. A platitude is a trite, meaningless, biased, or prosaic statement, often presented as fact-based, significant and original, when it is not. And 99% of all advertising is full of platitudes. For example, I always see "The customer comes first". And I always say – *prove it!*

Which leads us to the second biggest point about writing effective Yellow-Page ads... Making powerful, unique claims to demonstrate that you're better than any other solution that's available in the Yellow-Pages.

So how can you make a unique claim that demonstrates that "the customer comes first"? Here's a technique that's been used to great effect: The first thing you do is contact some of your past satisfied customers. Next, you ask them to write a quick one-paragraph testimonial about what they liked most about dealing with you. (It's easy to do this with the right strategy).

Then you put all those testimonials on a website.

Now, in your ad you can say, "You can even read what 117 satisfied customers had to say about our great products at..." and then put the website address in there. (Note: if that, or anything we discuss in this book is something you want done but don't know how to do, contact me and we can discuss your needs.)

Now, most people looking at the ad WON'T go to the webpage and read it. But it will have the effect of demonstrating to them that not only does the customer come first, but you have 117 of your own customers who say that you DO put them first.

You'll be the only ad in your category that can claim that, so in people's minds you'll be the preferred source if customer service is their main priority.

At any rate, your ad should contain at least one dramatic example of proof to validate your claims. It's best if you have specific numbers or facts to verify it, testimonials to show, and other powerful ways to demonstrate that you offer great service and goods.

...Something better than "In business since 1972!" So what??? I know a lot of bad companies that have stayed in business. Much better is "We've successfully helped over 10,678 clients in [your city] find the right blinds for their home."

So first come up with a powerful headline. Then, expand on that headline in your ad, and also throw in at least one dramatic example of proof to validate your claims.

Now you only have to do one final thing...

Have An Offer And A "Call-To-Action"

Every single ad you write should have an offer and a call-to-action to accept that offer. A call to action means that you tell them exactly what they should do after reading the ad.

Let me start with the best call to action, although it's also the most complicated one to set up.

What you ideally want is a continuing relationship with people who are interested in doing business with you, so if they are hesitant initially, further communication can get them in the door. The best way to do that is to offer something free to the prospect if they contact you. Here's a simple way to do that. Let's go back to the Blinds example...

The first thing you'd want to do is sit down and write a short 6-8 page *consumer awareness report* on "How To Pick The Most Beautiful Blinds For Your Home On A Shoestring Budget", or something similar.

Then just give them the best tips for getting the most value from their purchase.

What you're going to want to do next is take that report that you typed up on your computer and save it as a PDF. If you don't know how to do that, no sweat... just do a search on YouTube.com for "how to save a word doc to pdf".

Then, you'll want to setup an automated email followup system (an autoresponder account) at www.aweber.com. This allows you to have people sign up for an email list so you can send emails to your list in the future without having to email them one-by-one. You can even pre-load messages to go out automatically.

(Aweber is about $20/month, whereas MailChimp.com is a free alternative. However, most businesses and entrepreneurs much rather prefer Aweber, mostly because of its ease-of-use and straight forward simplicity. There is another way more robust and much more expensive system that I personally use, but Aweber is what I recommend you use starting out.)

Then, if they sign up for your list, they will automatically get delivered your free digital report on "How To Pick The Most Beautiful Blinds For Your Home On A Shoestring Budget". Not only that, but you can also use your autoresponder to send a few follow-up messages and/or special offers, automatically at certain intervals (twice per month, for example) to anyone who signs up.

Next, in your Yellow-Page ad you say, "If you'd like to get our free report on 'How To Pick The Most Beautiful Blinds For Your Home On A Shoestring Budget', then just go to www.YourWebsite.com/free-report".

This drives them to a page that explains that in order to get the report they just have to enter in their name and email into the form. (The form will be created automatically for you if you use Aweber.)

Of course, in the report you're going to want to put in your contact information so if they read it they can easily contact you and become your customer.

This is by far the best strategy but also the most complex. A simple strategy is to make a special "Yellow-Pages ad only" offer. In this case you say, "If you call us today to schedule an appointment, and mention you're calling because of the Yellow-Pages ad, we'll give you a 10%-off 'Yellow-Page' special deal!". In any case, you're enticing them to respond to your ad.

If you do all of the things that I outline in this chapter, then you're going to have an ad that is dramatically different, and better, than everyone else's ads, which is going to allow you to get dramatically better results!

How To Tear Down Customer Resistance

How many of the people who walk into your business, or who take an interest in your products and services, end up going ahead with a purchase? In sales, this is called a 'closing rate'.

To manage something, you first have to measure it. That way you know where it's at, so you know what you need to do to improve it. As Peter Drucker (probably the greatest management consultant of all time) said, "What is not measured, does not improve".

So here's a simple question you need to have an answer to: "If 10 prospects are interested in doing business with you, on average, how many out of those 10 end up doing business with you?" The percentage itself isn't important. In stores with a lot of visitor traffic, you can do 1 out of 10 and be fine. I have a website where I do 1 out of 100, and it's still good enough for me to make a great return on investment, because it takes hardly any time or effort. In some businesses, you need 5 out of 10 just to have a chance at making a profit.

What is important is knowing how to improve your percentages to a more "acceptable" range. So if you get 5 out of 10, do the math and see how much more you'd make if you got 6 out of 10.

Since they're already coming in the door, most of the work is done. You're just looking for those "little things" to get more people converted into customers.

There's a lot of different ways to improve your closing rate, and some are more complicated than others. I always look for the "80/20" factor in any given task.

In other words I'm looking for that one or two key things that will make most of the difference between someone purchasing from you or not. Here's some insight to help you discover that "vital one fact" that gives you a majority of your results...

Do you know what three things are required before a prospect becomes a customer? Knowing this will give you the answer you need. Here are the three things that are needed:

First, they have to want what you offer. Second, they have to have money to purchase it. Third, they have to believe with confidence that you'll actually come through on your end of the deal.

The more inclined they are to already want what you have, the easier it is to sell to them. The more money they have set aside for making consumer purchases, the easier it is to the sell to them. The more they believe that you actually will deliver on your offer, the easier it is to sell to them.

I have in front of me a big yellow phone book with ads in it. I'm going to flip through it and quote some phrases...

Here's one:

"Dependable & Quality Service"

> This is what I think – *Oh yeah!? Says who??*

"Friendly Service"

> I'm thinking – *Yeah. Right. I've heard that one before.*

"Value, Service & Convenience"

> Here are my thoughts – *PROVE IT!!*

Simply put, these are all just hollow phrases of platitudinal puffery, which everybody sheepishly uses. It's so easy to say those things, and saying those things means very little. I've actually called a business whose Yellow-Page ad said "friendly service" only to be treated quite rudely by the receptionist who answered the phone. (Guess someone forgot to tell her!)

So how do you go beyond mere puffery platitudes and actually prove your case that you're friendlier, more valuable, offer better service and are more dependable than every other option that your intended audience has available to them?

Well, I'll share with you one simple way to do this, which will drastically differentiate you from every competitor, both direct and indirect. As a bonus, it's also very simple to do, is extremely cost effective and when compiled, can be used in a variety of different outlets and mediums. What I'm talking about is *customer testimonials.*

The Selling Power Of Testimonials

If you want to increase your closing rates without resorting to any fancy tricks or learning a bunch of new skills, just start being an avid collector of testimonials.

I don't care what anyone else says, they work. Consider this – what if I told you I was the greatest marketing consultant of all time? Would you really believe me?

What if your friend called you up and told you I was the greatest marketing consultant? Then you might believe it. Right?

...Well, maybe.

But what if your lawyer, your chiropractor, your mother, your children's principal, the head of your trade association and the guy you buy cucumbers and bell peppers from at the local farmer's market told you I was the greatest marketing consultant of all time?

I bet you'd be really interested in sitting down and having a talk with me, wouldn't you? You'd probably think a great deal more of me than from me just calling you up and bragging about my skills.

This is such a simple principle, it makes me wonder – *why don't all businesses use testimonials?* I don't know why. Personally, I think it should be a requirement of doing business. That is because when it comes to raising your closing rates, it makes all the difference.

Now let me show you when, where, and how to get these killer testimonials that will increase the believability of your offers.

How To Become An Avid Testimonial Collector

If you go looking for opportunities to get testimonials, you'll find it's easy to begin collecting them.

The best opportunity is when your customer is 'in heat'. What I mean by this is that you've just done something that has "wowed" them. They might come in to pay their bill and say "I can't believe what a wonderful service you did. It's better than the last five people I've gone to!"

They are *in heat*! You say: "Thanks! Would it be okay if I shared your story with others who might be interested in our services as well?

It really helps us better serve our clients!"

Or, you can say: "Thanks. Would it be okay if I wrote down what you just said and shared it with others? It would mean a lot to me!" Then just write down really quickly what was said, and have them approve it.

Or you can simply say: "Thanks. Did you know that one of the best ways we get good clients just like you is by sharing the success stories of our past clients? Would it be okay if we quoted you in some of our marketing and sales communications?"

Don't make it harder than it has to be. The main process is: *get them when they're in a good mood*. Ask if you can have their permission to quote them and share their story. Then get their testimonial. That's it.

It's also smart if you ask them if you can share their name with others as well, just to be on the safe side.

If you do nothing else, just collect testimonials from customers who are in heat and have just expressed how appreciative they are of you and your services.

Another good time is when you "save the day". Did you do something for a customer that was out of the ordinary? Maybe you made a house call at 8:30 at night to fix an emergency, and didn't charge them the on-call after-hours rate. Or perhaps they wanted something that was supposedly discontinued, but you went the extra mile and tracked down what they were looking for.

Anytime you 'save the day', just ask them for a testimonial. In fact, make a point to intentionally look for opportunities to save-the-day, because it serves in your own self-interest and your business' best-interest.

If you go the extra mile, then you can be sure they'll give you one heck of a testimonial!

Once you get good at the first two, consider sending out a customer survey occasionally. Have them answer a few key questions. Then, retype those answers in a letter form, and ask them to sign off on it as a testimonial you can share with others.

There are more aggressive ways to get testimonials too, and for the most part in most cases, I would encourage you to be aggressive about getting them, especially after you've gotten the knack for getting the low hanging fruit.

Once you get used to asking your "in-heat customers" and those who you've "saved the day" for, experiment with actively seeking out testimonials to further prove your case.

How To Use Testimonials For Maximum Effect

I'll give you some examples you can literally knock off and use in your own business, and also that you can use to brainstorm your own ideas from.

Let's return to the yellow-book example. Instead of the typical puffery platitudes, your ad might include something that says:

"Look, any business can say that they care about the customer and that they are dependable and have high quality service. Instead of us touting our own horn, maybe you'd rather hear it from some of our customers themselves. Just call our 'satisfied customer hotline' to hear a pre-recorded message of what our customers think about our services: 1-800-555-1234, ext.4"

You know how much a voicemail account costs? Something like $3 per month. For less than $3 a month from Kall8.com, you can have a dedicated hotline, either a toll-free number or local, with a recording of your best customers. How do you get these recorded?

Well, let's just think about this a bit... Perhaps you have your sales reps call your customers a few days after the sale. Explain to the customer that for quality issues, would it be okay if you recorded the call?

This can be done relatively inexpensively with a digital phone recorder that you can get from Dynametric.com or from UsbCallRecord.com (for slightly larger or more technically sophisticated office-environment phone and PBX systems), and for smaller businesses through an online service such as CallFire.com.

Another couple alternatives is to use the Pamela Call Recorder plugin with Skype (which costs about $30), or use a call recording app with your smartphone. (For Android use AndroRec Call Recorder; it's free. For iPhone, use CallRec.me, it's also free. Or just do a search in the App Store for Call Recorder and choose whichever best suits your preferences.)

Then, ask what their thoughts were on the service or for the product. At the end, ask them if it would be okay if you shared their thoughts with others who might be interested in your products or services.

That's just one way to get your testimonials recorded. There are of course many other ways though. Now you have a tool – you have people talking about how good you are. You can now put this pre-recorded message into all of your marketing communications, and your believability and credibility will go through the roof!

Here's something else you might want to consider – gathering up a "testimonial book"...

Do you know of ANY salesperson who has a testimonial book? Hmm... Wouldn't that distinguish you from every other competitor out there? I think it would – and it's a really good way to do so.

Let's say you really went the extra mile and totally knock it out of the park for a customer. They were so happy they called you up and thanked you personally, and said they were so impressed with you, how you went above and beyond the call of duty.

Well how about this – you ask them if it would be okay to feature them as a "case study" in your next marketing piece.

Then you could write an advertisement that looks like an article, where you simply tell the story of what you did for this customer. This type of promotional is about a million times more effective than all the "BUY MY SHIT!" advertisements you currently see everywhere.

At the very least, you should include some testimonials in your advertising, just to enhance your claims.

One of my clients took it an extra step after taking my advice from a strategy session we had together, to go as far as recording all her customer testimonials on video. Then, when someone didn't purchase the first time they came into her store, five days later they'd get a disc in the mail that contained all these wonderful customer testimonial videos.

Needless to say, a lot of people came back and ended up purchasing who otherwise would not have.

The Anatomy Of A Great Testimonial

Now, some people have tried testimonials and have told me that they don't work. Well, it reminds me of a close family friend telling me a few years ago that her DVD player didn't work. I asked her, "Did you plug it in?"

– *"Well DUH, of course I plugged it in."*

Then I asked her, "Did you plug in the red, yellow and white cables from the DVD player to the TV?"

– *"...Oh. Oops!"* ☺

Testimonials are like anything else – if you do them half-assed then they probably won't work. In order to do them right, you must know what a good testimonial looks like.

Here's a bad testimonial:

> "You did a great job, thanks!"

Here's a killer testimonial:

> "You responded to our call and were at our house in 7 minutes. The last guys took 2.5 hours. Not only that, you helped us save 15% off the cost. I'm definitely going to refer you to my mother and our next-door neighbor. Thanks a bunch!"
> ~ Name,
> Occupation,
> City, Prov/State

The difference is obvious. Bad testimonials are bland, generic, ambiguous, and overall really don't say anything. Good testimonials are specific and give you hard facts.

I love it when someone says to me: "I read your book on Tuesday, and by Thursday morning I did one thing I learned on page 19 that resulted in me making $15,867.13 in profit by the following Monday. Thanks Jayson, you're awesome!". That's a far better testimonial than "your ideas helped me make more money".

Not only is specificity needed, but it's good to have a name, occupation and location. Otherwise people will think that maybe you're just making up the testimonials yourself, even though that is illegal (which is why audio and video testimonials are best).

Also, there are other things that can influence your testimonials. What's better: five testimonials featured in your ads all from white males aged 43, or a mix of ages, races and both genders?

Well, it depends. If your product or service specifically targets only white males who are 43 years old, then of course it's a good idea. Chances are though that it targets a wide variety of audiences, so you'll want testimonials from a wide variety of people.

Lastly, as humans we're hardwired by nature to trust authority. That's why testimonials from scientists, doctors, nurses, fire-fighters, and other professional or esteemed positions tend to have more pull than regular testimonials. Just think how much more credible a testimonial is from a Senior Rocket Engineer than from a McDonald's Drive-through Attendant.

So set a plan – come up with the different ways you're going to capture and use testimonials, and make sure everybody in your business starts to become a testimonial collector. It's one of the easiest ways to increase your sales closing percentage.

Word Of Mouth Advertising

The idea is that you should be generating a large portion of your new customers by marketing to existing customers.

There are several reasons why this is smart to do. First, quality attracts quality. Psychologists say that you are basically a combination of your five closest friends. In other words, people will refer people who are similar to them.

So if you have a big spender, then guess what? They'll probably refer other big spenders. Every good customer should be actively pursued for a referral because they'll usually generate other customers of equal quality and value.

Most marketing is usually met with skepticism too. That's because you are often tooting your own horn. But what if someone else was tooting your horn for you?

Know this – people are more likely to believe in you if someone else endorses your quality, than if you yourself brag about your own qualities.

What you're really doing is leveraging off of someone else's credibility. People who take the recommendations of their friends are now coming to you with a preconceived notion that you're already quality – before you even have to open your mouth.

Finally, word of mouth marketing is target marketing. Basically, you're only going to be getting people who already are in the market for what you're offering. Mass marketing does not have this effect. If you run an ad on TV, you're getting *everybody* who watches TV.

But with referral marketing, you're pretty much only getting people who are already great matches to your products or services. This means your closing rate will go up without having to learn one single bit of salesmanship. You're just getting people who are already more likely to say "yes" before they even enter into the store. If you're not already relying heavily on referrals, you should be; it has an immensely high R.O.I.

Okay, know my rule of thumb when it comes to referral marketing – every good customer should get three direct chances to refer someone else to you.

I have found in order to get the best results, you have to ask someone three times to make a referral on your behalf. If you do nothing else, you should do this.

However, to really make it effective, there are two more things you need to do… Make it easy for them to refer, and make it worthwhile to refer. I'm going to describe how to do all of this and more, as I outline what I have found time and time again to be a profit pulling monster when it comes to referral systems.

The Referral System, Step By Step

First, get your metrics in order. How much money can you afford to spend on marketing for next month? Whatever it is, devote the largest portion of it to your referral marketing. So step one, find your budget.

Now, the specific plan I'm going to lay out to you is going to cost around $8 per person to perform. So if you have a budget of $8000 for marketing, then you can reach 1000 people.

Start small and scale up – that's my advice.

Don't spend too much upfront until you get back some reliable figures, and you can do some testing.

Since this is a system, every dollar you spend will be tracked and traced back to determine your return on investment. Remember... *What is measured, improves.*

Here's how it works... Someone comes in and buys from you. Immediately the next day, you send them out a letter in the mail. You thank them, ask for the referral, make it easy for them to refer, and then make it worth their while.

The most important part here is that it's in their best interest to refer others to you. For that to happen, first and foremost you must have provided quality and value. So I'm going to assume you're performing good service and living up to your end of the deal.

Second, gifts work wonders. My favourite kind of gifts are those that either cost me nothing or very little, but have a huge perception of value. Without a doubt, there is one gift I can consistently create for basically nothing, and it always does the trick.

Coupon books.

It works like this – you go around to different business owners and tell them that you want to make sure your customers shop locally. As a thank-you gift for your customers, you'd like to give them coupons or special offers from other local merchants, so you're providing your customers with value, and also keeping business local.

Then you simply ask them if they have any coupons or anything they'd like to contribute to your "customer gift-book".

Almost every business owner you talk to will take you up on this. Why? Well, most businesses are not good at marketing, and to make up for it they always have a special deal going on, or are willing to do anything if it means getting a few more customers in the store.

Besides, you only need to get like 15 or 20 different coupons anyway to make a great gift-book. You can get this all done in a few hours.

So now you have a great gift that you can give to anybody who sends a referral your way. How much did it cost you? Just the cost to print up the coupons and mail them. So you just made a gift of high perceived value (*everybody loves coupons!*) that costs you about $1 to create and a few hours of sweat equity, thus, it's worth their while. Now let's take a look at what the first referral letter should look like:

"Dear Jane Customer,

The other day you made a purchase from our store, and we just wanted to say thank-you from the bottom of our hearts for doing business with us. If there is anything you ever need in the future, please don't hesitate to call us up and ask. We'll see what we can do!

You may not know it, but the lifeline of our business comes from referrals. If you happen to know anyone else who could use our services, I'd be extremely happy to sit down and talk with them to see if we might be able to help them in any way.

And, if it so happens that the person you refer becomes our customer, then as a token of my appreciation I will send you my special "valued customer gift-book"!

This special "valued customer gift-book" has a total of over $250 worth of coupons for discounts from local businesses of all kinds!

I'll give the same gift to your friend as well.

It's really easy to refer someone to us. I've enclosed two of my business cards with your name written on the back of them. Just give them to anyone who you think could use our services. Just have them present the business card when they come in, so we know it was you that referred them!

Anyway, I just wanted to say thanks again for deciding to go with us!

Thanks,
Joe Business-Owner"

There is a lot of psychology that is going on in this first letter that I don't want you to miss.

First, it's personal and it's sincere. How many businesses have you bought something from in the last sixty days that sent you a personal thank-you letter in the mail?

Hmmm... maybe only one or two you say?

So imagine what kind of impact that your letter has when it lands in your customer's mailbox. Big impact. It says you care. Do you know why most people leave a service provider?

A few die. Some move away. Others leave because of an unresolved complaint. A handful will be stolen away by a competitor. Now add all those up, and guess what?

It usually only comes to 32% of all total customers who leave you. So what about the other 68%? They leave simply because you never have taken the time to recognize them as something more than a customer.

Pop quiz – If you had an unresolved complaint, a direct competitor in your store trying to steal your customer, or the opportunity to let someone who purchased from you know you care... and you can only choose one option... which one should you choose?

You better choose the third option, right? Of course, because roughly only 9% leave because of competition, and only 14% leave because of unresolved complaints.

If you do nothing else but keep in contact with your past customers and treat them as your friends, or at the very least just acknowledge them once in a while, you'll be putting the "golden handcuffs" on two-thirds of your customers, which will allow you to keep selling to them again and again.

If you get nothing else out of the referral letter, you will get that personal communication that will separate you from 90% of all businesses, and almost every single one of your competitors.

The second thing that letter does is conveys your expectations. You expect all your customers to refer others. Most people don't refer simply because they don't know you want them to refer. In fact, I've seen customers come up and tell a client – "Heck, I thought you already had enough customers, I didn't know you could take on more..." You should've seen that business owner slap his forehead.

Once people know that you want them to refer their inner-circle to you, you automatically increase the chances they will refer, even if it isn't immediate.

Again, I've had people hold on to business cards for two or three years before they gave one to someone else.

Also notice the casual tone of the letter. People prefer doing business with friends and peers, not faceless corporations.

Finally, it shows you care. The above letter basically says, *"Hey, I know you're busy and I know you need to look out for your own self-interests... That's why I've gone the extra mile to make it in your own self-interest to refer others to me!"*

Ideally, you don't want to take the above letter word for word. You want to fill in "our services" with your actual services and so forth. But I give you permission to take most of the above verbatim and use it as yours.

But don't stop there. After the first letter is sent out... wait 10-15 days. If you haven't gotten a referral from them yet, then send them letter-two:

"Dear Jane Customer,

A few weeks ago I sent you a letter thanking you for your purchase. I hope you got everything you wanted out of it and more.

Remember – if you ever need help with anything, I'm only a phone call away.

We've also sent out several "customer gift-books" in the last few weeks to our valued customers who referred one of their friends to us.

I know things can get busy, and sometimes stuff can get misplaced in the shuffle.

To make sure you don't miss out on your own special customer gift-book, I've sent you two more business cards with your name printed on the back – just in case you misplaced the last two I sent you.

Just give those to a friend in need, if you think we can help them, and we'll mail you your "customer gift-book" pronto!

Once again, I just wanted to say thanks for being our customer, and we hope that we can continue to provide you with more service in the years to come.

Thanks,
Joe Business-Owner"

Here's what I know about marketing – one-shot advertising is not very effective. (Understatement of the year?)

It's not that people don't want to act on your offers; a lot of them do. What happens is that the day-to-day details take over, and what they intend on doing ends up getting pushed to the back of their mind. What this letter does is thank them again, puts you in front of them again, and basically lets them off the hook – hey, it wasn't their fault. You know they're busy people!

It also gives you another excuse to send them two more business cards. Plus it offers some social proof – "Hey, everybody else is referring…"

Every time we track these campaigns, we usually find something like this – we get 3% to refer off the first letter. We get 4% to refer off the second letter, and we get 2% to refer off the third. Now 2-4% may not sound like much from the outset, but in any case, all mailings are quite profitable.

Now think – if we just stopped after the first time, we'd get a 3% response. But instead we got a 9% response! In most scenarios, it almost always plays out that the second letter will work the best. Who knows why – it just usually does.

Now those who didn't respond to letter number one, and don't respond to letter number two, will get, after 10-15 more days, the third and last letter:

"Dear Jane Customer,

Hope everything is going great for you!

The reason I'm writing to you today is because I had a few "customer gift-books" left over and didn't want them to go to waste.

I had one specifically set aside for you, so I have enclosed it with this letter. It is just our way of saying 'thanks for being a great customer'.

Also, just in case you lost the last cards in the laundry or something, I've put in two more business cards with your name printed on the back.

Just pass them on to a friend if they're ever in need of any services or products we offer. We'll make sure to treat them right.

Thanks,
Joe Business-Owner"

Now, I don't want you to confuse the technique with the strategy. This works because:

1. It puts you in front of them three times.

2. It conveys the expectation that they will refer.

3. It is personal and friendly.

4. It is easy to do.

5. It is in their own best interest.

You don't have to do the coupon gift-book to leverage this kind of strategy. Sometimes instead I'll just purchase tickets for a special upcoming local event, or even complimentary dinners at a nice restaurant.

Lastly, a few more pointers – make your letters look like personal letters. This means, when you design the layout, don't put some fancy "brochure" feel into it.

Just picture how you'd design the letter if you were going to sit down and write someone a personal note from a typewriter.

Also, when you get this system in place, you'll get some numbers. You might find for every 5 customers you do this for, you get 1 referral in the next 30 days. Okay, do that math – let's say that your average sale netted you $1000 in profit.

For creating and mailing the letters, it cost you $100. That's a 10 to 1 return on investment! Try getting that with other types of one-off advertising.

This type of marketing also allows you to test... What would happen if you altered the gift? What would happen if you offered the same gift to both your customer and to the person they're going to refer?

You can literally test every element you want, and know what is working and what isn't working.

This means you can figure out the exact combination of steps for getting the greatest return on investment.

Split-testing in all of your marketing initiatives (not just for getting testimonials) is always a very good, very profitable habit to get into nonetheless.

How To Put Your Profits On Steroids

Let's say in your backyard, there was a huge amount of oil under your ground. We're talking millions of dollars worth.

Would that make you rich? Not if you didn't know about it! You could live your whole life sitting on "liquid gold" and be none-the-wiser.

However, if I came up to you and told you about it, and showed you beyond a shadow of doubt that there was oil and you drilled for it, then you'd be abundantly rich.

In most small businesses, there DOES exist a situation that is similar to the oil-well example above. Most small business owners are sitting on a potential fortune and they don't even realize it.

In this section I'm going to share with you what is perhaps the single most effective strategy for mining the "hidden gold" that is likely to exist in your business.

The Forgotten "Rule" Of An Obscure Italian Economist

In 1906 a man by the name of Vilfredo Pareto discovered something unusual about the Italian economy – 80% of the wealth was controlled by 20% of the population.

Was this just an anomaly? Turns out it wasn't. In Britain he found the same thing to be true and found it to be true in pretty much all economies. But what's interesting is that this unequal distribution exists outside of economies as well.

For example, studies have shown in general that:

- 80% of all traffic accidents are committed by 20% of drivers.

- 80% of crimes are committed by 20% of the population.

- 80% of a company's output comes from 20% of its employees.

And most importantly of all...

- ***80% of your profits come from only 20% of your customers!***

This is almost always true. So what does that mean for you?

Simple: if you can isolate who those top 20-percent'ers are, and then come up with a marketing plan that will attract more customers like those "top 20-percent'ers" and also create additional products, services and offers for your "top 20-percent'ers", then...

You should be able to, very easily, add 20% or more to your bottom-line profits within the next 90 days.

Where To Start

In an ideal situation, you've kept track of your past customers' purchases, so you can access their records. What you want to do is go through and first isolate customers who have spent the most money with you.

Now, that doesn't necessarily mean that they are your most profitable customers.

They are just your highest grossing customers. Unfortunately, gross does not always mean more profitable. However, it's a good place to start.

After you find your highest grossing customers, then analyze your profit margin on those customers, to narrow it down even more. To make it easy for you, come up with your 50 "highest grossing customers", and out of those 50, arrange them in order of most profitable, in terms of percentages.

Now take your 20 "most profitable" customers, and analyze them. What we are looking for here are their *demographics* and their *psychographics*.

Demographics are things such as:

- Size of Household

- Annual Income Earned

- Age

- Gender

- Geographical Location

Psychographics are:

- What clubs they belong to

- What their hobbies and interests are

- Their Values

- Their Opinions

- Lifestyle attributes and other behavior attributes

In other words, you are trying to isolate their "culture" – so to speak.

How can this be helpful to you? Well, let's say you analyze your results and find out that, on average, your most profitable customers are typically:

White, aged 45-50, have 2-3 children, are married, live on the northwest side of town, make between $75,000 to $100,000 per year, are active in the community, especially with charitable events, typically play a lot of golf and/or tennis, are Progressive Conservatives for example, and often take 2-3 vacations a year.

That's some valuable information! For starters, did you know you can rent a list in your area with those "selects" (select is just mailing-house industry jargon for different attributes).

Yes, for a fee you could get a list of all the people in your city that are between 45-50, living in a certain postal code, making an annual income of $75,000 to $100,000 per year. And that's just a few of the "selects" you can specify. You can even go deeper if you wish.

These are the type of prospects you want to invest your money marketing to! While past results do not necessarily guarantee future behavior, they are about as good an indicator to go by as any. The point is, if that type of customer was profitable to you in the past, it stands to reason similar people who fit that description will also be extremely profitable for you NOW.

Then what do you do? The best thing is to create a direct-mail campaign and send a letter to each name on the list you rented, making them a special offer.

You want to write an advertisement that is personable, explains the benefits of your services, and makes a special "introductory offer" to get them into your place of business.

Even better is if, in those advertisements, you talk about things like golf and tennis, taking vacations, saying things that Progressive Conservatives are known to agree with, talking about charitable events.

This all helps build rapport with the prospect. You just have to tie those things to your sales message and offer in some creative way.

And that's just one simple example of how to make the "80/20" rule work in your favour.

Here's an even better example: Look into your customer records of your most profitable customers and ask yourself, "What services and goods can I offer them that they don't currently have, but would be complementary to purchases they've made in the past?"

If someone is a very profitable customer to you, it usually means they like doing business with you, need a lot of what you have to offer, trust you, and often think of you as the "go-to" solution for problems related to your area of service and expertise.

So if you have a good recommendation that could help bring them value to their life, and is a perfect fit for something you've offered them in the past, you're likely to meet with success.

Here's how you can maximize your efforts: Start with your top 20 customers. What you want to do is write them a PERSONAL letter to each of them.

Start with talking about how you were analyzing your past records and noticed that they have been a very good customer, and that you value their business. Then say you also noticed something that may be a benefit, and since they've been a good customer, you're going to give them a special deal next time they come into the store and purchase something from you. Give them specific examples, such as:

> "I noticed you purchased X from us. Well a new product that we just got the rights to distribute, complements X perfectly.

> So if you come in within the next 2 weeks I can give you a special deal of 40% off the shelf price. This is just my way of saying thanks for being such a valuable customer."

Another strategy to consider is the referral strategy. Think about this: People typically hang around others who share their same values and beliefs. This is a perfect way to attract new customers who are likely to be just as profitable as your past "most profitable customers" are.

In this case, you'd send your best customers a letter, and let them know that you're making them a "valued customer special offer" if they recommend someone to your business, and you'll give their referrals a "preferred VIP discount" or "preferred VIP treatment", since they came from a highly valued source.

People love to refer when this is the case. It makes them look good in front of their friends, and a lot of people get value in that. It's also great for you, because word of mouth advertising is some of the most profitable and highest value advertising there is.

Also, if you can just get these referrals into the door and have them start a buying relationship with you, chances are they will continue to buy from you in the future. Thus you will get more than just a one-off purchase; you may get a customer for life with a high lifetime value.

There are several other very powerful strategies you can use to get a lot of profits from a just a little list of "most profitable customers". This is an area I excel at, and if you'd like to further explore this and other ideas, if you qualify, I am open to having a conversation with you about this in an initial consultation session.

During this 35-minute marketing-strategy analysis, either I or one of my Account Executives from Consulting Experts Online will review your existing marketing material and strategies, and learn what your marketing and business-growth goals are. With this information, we will go back to our office where myself or one of my Expert Marketing Consultants will analyze all the gaps and missed opportunities in your current marketing program. You will also be shown where opportunities with "Marketing Leverage" exist and how you can take advantage of them.

To see if you might be a good fit to do business with my company and schedule your free Marketing-Leverage Analysis Consultation (valued at $495), just contact my office at **1-800-923-9495** or **Yes@CEO-HQ.com** to apply. Not everyone will qualify to take advantage of this however. I need to make sure that my team and I, and my client and their company, will be a good fit for us all to do business together. Be aware also that I do offer my clients the privilege of exclusivity, meaning in most cases, I will only work with one company per industry per geographical market area. (So don't wait!)

Centers-of-Influence Marketing

Normal advertising SUCKS.

Why? Because *normal advertising* will get you *normal results*. You don't become an industry leader or a dominant presence by doing things the "normal" way.

Most small businesses advertise in the Yellow-Pages. I think you're going to find Yellow-Page advertising is going to become weaker and weaker, because more people now use the internet to find their information, and the numbers are only skyrocketing.

In fact, according to ComScore Networks, 54% of North Americans have replaced their phonebooks for local-based searches on the internet. That's roughly 189 million people who tossed out their phonebooks for the internet.

Besides, almost all Yellow-Page ads look the same. Hmmm... could it be because they're all designed by the same people? So, everybody is normal?

Newspaper advertising is also failing. Just look at how many newspaper companies have closed their doors over the last few years. And the numbers are climbing. But let's look at it – again almost all the ads look the same. Could it be because they're all designed yet again by the same people? Hmmm... If everything looks normal, everybody gets normal results.

Finally, consider this – you're advertising in the same place as your competitors. That's kind of dumb isn't it? I'd rather advertise in a vacuum where I'm the only choice (as long as even just some of my ideal prospects and target-market are hanging out there, that is).

You have to think outside the box. I fashion myself as a collector of good ideas. I look for those different ways of advertising that don't get normal results... but rather get *extraordinary results*.

What I'm about to show you is going to give you a far greater return than normal advertising ever will.

It will also dramatically enhance the relationship you have with your fellow business owners and finally it'll just make others think you're some sort of genius because of your innovation.

I'm talking about *Centers-of-Influence marketing*. Here's the premise – instead of going out hunting down your ideal prospects, what would happen if you already went to where a bunch of them hang out, and just put your sign up in front of them? You're going to where they already are, instead of picking them up "one by one" in the newspaper, on the television, or in the Yellow-Pages.

Okay, so here's what you're going to do – you're going to come up with a bunch of different places where your ideal customers frequent in large numbers. Then you're going to construct an offer that will allow you to siphon those ideal customers off into your own sales funnel. And, it's only going to cost you a small "toll booth" fee to do this, which you will only pay out of a portion of the profits you're generating.

Before we get into the details, let's take a second to talk about 'target-marketing'. Say you and I both owned a pizza place. I would only need one competitive advantage, and I could win virtually every single customer. I'd give you all other advantages, because, when totaled, they still wouldn't give you a chance.

Yes, I would give you the best ingredients. I'd give you the best employees. I'd give you the coolest store layout ever. I'd even give you the best location in the wealthiest part of town in the wealthiest city of the country. But I'd only ask for one thing... I'd only ask that all my customers be nearly dying of hunger!

When someone is hungry, they don't care what your store looks like, if you have an ultra-polished image and professional designs. They don't care if you have good service. They don't care if the food even tastes good. They are just so hungry that they'll pay anything and eat anything to quell that hunger.

Perhaps that isn't the most realistic example ever, but it is very illustrative of the topic and quite applicable. What target-marketing does is it isolates and focuses your efforts on singling out those who are "hungriest" for whatever you offer.

Let me make it real to you. Let's say you're in the retail flooring business. Okay, now people who buy flooring... what else do they tend to need that complements that?

Well, a lot of people who need flooring also need paint. What if you had a majority of the paint stores sending their customers who also needed flooring your way?

Since I market to small and medium-sized businesses to offer my marketing consultation services, where do I go? Well, I start with the local accountants, because they help a lot of business owners with their taxes.

I also go to the heads of trade associations that small business owners would be a member of (like the Chamber of Commerce, for example), and volunteer for free to give speeches where I can share my expertise on how to get more customers and increase profits.

I go to attorneys that help people form corporations, and attorneys who specialize in helping small businesses. See what I'm doing here?

I'm finding a complementary, non-competitive business entity that already attracts the "hungry" customers that I'm in search of. Instead of having to find those clients myself, I'm leveraging the efforts of my centers of influence.

Now, here's how to NOT make this work. Go up to one of these centers of influence and say, "Hey, why don't you tell your customers to come to me when they need X." That is just stupid, lazy, and lame, lame, lame!

You have to make it make sense for them to refer others to you before they will. What's an easy way to do this? Why not say, "Hey, I know from time to time you have customers that also need my services. So how do you feel about this... Every time you send someone over my way, and they become my customer, I give you X% of the sale?". Warning – in some industries, it's actually illegal to do this. And since I'm no lawyer, check the laws first to make sure that you can legally leverage this strategy. I'm just giving you one example here. There are other ways you can reward them too.

For example, send customers to them in return. It could be as simple as making a stack of fliers up to put in their business, and they do likewise to distribute at your business. Now it's a "referral revolving door" and more importantly... it's a win-win situation.

Here's how you can make it work for you. First, pull out the Yellow-Pages if you haven't already trashed it. Go through the index, and each time you find a category that would be complementary to your business, write it down.

Get 5-10 different "complementary industries", and then pick the top 3 businesses in each of those industries. Now you have a list of 15-30 businesses to approach.

Second, create your "irresistible-offer" for these businesses. If you can give them a cash incentive for a referral, then consider that as your offer. Or come up with something equally enticing that answers their number one question – *"So what? What's in it for me?"*

Another thing you can do here is to give a special offer just for their customers. It could be a discount, or something extra they get for free that you would normally charge for. This way, the "What's in it for me?" is that their customers will like them more, because it looks like the owner went to bat and negotiated a special deal just for them.

How many businesses could you do this with? Well, as many as you would like. This can take care of the new customer acquisition end of things, especially when you combine it with referral marketing.

Think about it... you could easily get ten businesses that were complementary to you to promote for you for some sort of incentive.

For some, it might just be that you put up some fliers at the counter, with a special "freebie" just for their customers. For other businesses, it might be a customer exchange. You send customers their way if they send customers your way. For others still, it might work to downright pay them a cut of the sales.

In any case, realize the importance behind this – most of the cost for customer acquisition will only be paid *after the customer is acquired.*

You pay a percentage of the sale... after the sale is made. You get referrals because you refer.

This truly takes the risk out of advertising, because you'll only pay for it if it works. – Not a bad deal!

Stop Making These 3 Costly Mistakes

Do you know what the most profitable skill is for running a small business?

It's not keeping the shelves stocked. It's not managing employees. It's not even having a good product.

No. The most important skill is *strategically marketing your business*. Why? Well, the only time you can bring money into your business is if you sell something. You can't stock the shelves unless you have money to buy the stuff to put on the shelves.

And you can't pay your employees unless you have money come in the business from selling stuff. A good product might as well be a piece of junk in a box if nobody knows it exists.

That's where strategic marketing (and not just one-shot advertising) comes into effect. It's how you communicate to the public that you have a great product or service, that you offer a great consumer experience and that they should buy from or do business with you, rather than one of your competitors.

Marketing is also the most misunderstood (and like I already mentioned, the most essential, most crucial, most important and most profitable) skill in any business.

Most business owners think that advertising and marketing are the same thing, and that all they need to do is 'advertise' their business so they can just 'get their name out there'. (Sound familiar?) This couldn't be any further from the truth. You see, there is a huge difference between marketing and advertising.

Advertising is essentially just all about getting your name out to as many people as possible. For the most part, you should think of regular branding and advertising as an expensive, wasteful, shotgun approach with no real or efficient way of knowing if it will actually produce any PROFITABLE results and is very difficult, and often impossible, to track what is working if you ever, for the entire life of your business, engage in more than one advertising campaign – whether presently, in the past, or in the future.

Unless you use tracking codes and separate tracking phone numbers for each advertising method (which I actually do implement for all my clients), or are absolutely compulsive about asking each and every one of your leads and customers how they heard about you – and then keeping track of everything with the use of complicated spreadsheets and having advanced mathematical formulas, macros and pivot-tables built into your spreadsheets, you really have no way of knowing which advertising method is returning profitable results, or any results.

It doesn't matter what kind of results any marketing or advertising gets you if those results aren't undoubtedly PROFITABLE results!

Think about it, what good does it do your business at all, just to 'get your name out there' or have some flashy designed branding material – if without a shadow of a doubt your numbers can't prove on paper to an accountant (or more importantly, to you) that you're getting a positive return on your investment?

Marketing on the other hand, – or rather, what is known as 'Performance-Based Marketing' (which is what I specialize in) – when done effectively, is so much more cost-effective because it's so much easier to produce profitable results, and to be able to track each of your marketing efforts so you can know which is producing what results, and if those results are profitable or not.

You see, unlike advertising which is all about taking the shotgun approach to get your name out to as many people as possible, and for the most part is nearly impossible to significantly measure any revenue or results it's responsible for producing, my approach to marketing is all about getting your message out to as many people as possible... *who're ALREADY SEARCHING* for the type of products or services that you offer.

With performance-based marketing, it has to produce revenue; bottom-line. You also must be able to measure the results for continually optimizing and increasing the effectiveness and profitability of your marketing. It's so true: *that which is measured, improves.*

Because if it's not performing, why continue with it? That's exactly why I feel so strongly that performance-based marketing is exponentially more powerful and more important to a business than traditional branding or advertising ever could be.

However, poor marketing (according to the Direct-Marketing Association) is the reason why 65% of new businesses close their doors after just two years, and why over 85% of businesses don't make it eight years before going under.

Since most of your competition does not understand how to do marketing properly, to bring in amazing results in little to no time, just knowing a few simple things will put you at a great advantage. After all, in the land of the blind, the person with one eye is KING.

And hopefully by now you've picked up more than just a few simple insights!

I'm now going to give you the *three most powerful* – and most profitable – marketing strategies *EVER*, so you can become the KING in your area...

Mistake #1:
Focusing On Getting New Customers

Yes, you read that right. New customers can be the most expensive people in the world to find, attract into your place of business, and then convert into customers.

To help you understand this, let me demonstrate to you a powerful fact...

There are **only 3 ways** to increase your profits. The first way is to increase your number of customers. If Timmy has a lemonade stand and sells 100 cups per day to 100 people and makes $0.10 per cup for a total of $10 a day in profit... If Timmy figures out a way to get 200 people to buy a cup, he has just doubled his profits.

But that's not the only way Timmy can double his profit. What if, instead, he figures out a way for his customers to purchase two cups of lemonade each? Then, with the same number of customers, he can double his profits.

Or, what if Timmy also offers something that is complimentary to the lemonade... such as a slice of watermelon? Then, if a certain percentage ALSO buys a piece of watermelon when he sells them lemonade, he can double his business.

So did you get them all? Are you able to tell me now what they are? Well just in case you didn't, I'll help you...

Quick review of the only three ways to grow your profits:

1. Get more customers;
2. Get the same customers to purchase more stuff;
3. Get the same customers to purchase more often.

Of the three, which is the most profitable? Well, let's look at it like this. Let's say you spend $5000 a year on a Yellow-Page ad, and it brings you in 100 prospective customers.

You have paid $50 for each person that has come into your store who might purchase from you. That is a *static cost*. You pay that $50 if they buy nothing from you, or if they buy everything in the store.

So what if you could increase the average transaction value of each customer by just $10? What would it cost you? Usually, nothing but a few minutes of creative thought. You've already paid $50 to get them in the store so you might as well maximize their value. Right?

In Timmy's case, he "cross-sold" them on some watermelon. It's just a matter of creatively picking complimentary goods and using the right language to get the highest number of people to say Yes to buy something in addition to what they originally came in to the store to purchase.

McDonald's simply asks: "Do you want fries with that?"

Extra cost for McDonald's to do that: 2 seconds of training for the employee, and 2 seconds for the employee to say it to each customer.

The result: an overall bump of about $0.08 in profit per customer. And when you have "over 1 billion served", that's a lot of extra profit for them.

So... Rule #1: spend more of your marketing budget and time on figuring out how to get customers who have purchased from you in the past, or your new prospects, to PURCHASE MORE from you!

Often times, the last thing you need is more customers.

Whatever problems you currently have in your business usually multiplies when you bring more customers into the funnel. Instead, figure out how to get MORE from the same number of customers.

This leads to Rule #2: figure out how to get past customers to make more frequent purchases from you!

Here's *everything* required in order to make your marketing work:

- They have to KNOW you exist;

- They have to WANT and can afford what you offer;

- They have to TRUST you.

See, new customers first need to hear about you. But that's not enough. They also have to be in the market for what you offer. It's hard to sell squirrel clothing, or ice cream to Eskimos... ya' know? Finally, they have to trust you enough to exchange their hard earned dollars for the value you promise to deliver to them.

Past customers, on the other hand, already know you exist, already have demonstrated that they need at least some of what you offer, and at least at one point in their life they trusted you enough to exchange their dollars for the value you promised them.

All else being equal, who do you think is going to be more inclined to say yes to your next offer? A stranger, or someone who knows you and is likely to be comfortable dealing with you again?

I think the answer is obvious. Before we go into how to get past-customers to increase the frequency of which they purchase from you, let's first deal with increasing the average purchasing size from each customer...

Mistake #2:
Not Using Cross-Sells,
Up-Sells and "Package" Selling

We already discussed 'cross-sells' with the *"do you want fries with that?"* example. So what does this mean for your business? The first thing you need to do is implement your own cross-sells.

Here's a simple way to do that... Look at your 5 to 7 most popular sellers in your business. Each one of them should have a cross-sell. For example in the flooring business, when people buy carpeting, you should also have a special offer for them to buy "spot remover" along with their carpeting.

You can even give them a special "purchase discount" because you don't need as high of margins since you have ALREADY PAID (in marketing and advertising, such as with our previous $50 per lead example) to attract them to come in the door and purchase from you.

So select your five biggest sellers, and find other items that you can offer with them that complement these main purchases (just like how fries compliment a cheeseburger and an extra-big size compliments a meal-deal).

Then, (this is crucial here) just create a quick script to use and train your employees to use this technique.

It could be something as simple as "Would you be interested in receiving a special 60% purchaser discount on spot-remover to complement your flooring purchase today?" Really, anything is better than nothing.

Based on tests, even a weak attempt at a cross-sell works 6%-20% of the time.

The point being is that cross-sells have almost no hard cost at all to implement, so why not do it?

The second thing is the up-sell. This is where you try to offer them a more premium version of what they are ready to purchase. Let's return to the flooring example:

There are different pads you can put under your carpet. There is the basic pad, often made of several different materials that are bonded together, thus making it cheaper to sell to the client. Then there is "prime" pad, which is solid, more durable, makes the flooring last longer, but is more expensive.

In this case, when putting together an offer for the customer, you'd want to say something like, "Would you like to invest a little bit more to make this carpet last 6 years longer – and feel much more comfortable under your feet?"

Then, you simply explain why buying the upgraded version of the padding is a better option for them.

Now think about it – if your markup is the same for both types of padding, then you'll make more money if you sell them the more expensive carpet pad.

Example: let's say you make 50% profit on each pad you sell. If a customer needs 100 square yards of the basic pad, and that sells for $4.50 per square yard, then you just sold $450 of materials, of which $225 is profit to you.

But what if you could've bumped them up to the premium pad that sells for $7.50 per square yard? Now that's $750 in material sold, of which $375 is profit to you. That's an increase of $150 for just a few moments of additional sales conversation.

Again, all you have to do is come up with a simple script, and a simple way to demonstrate why the little bit of extra cost involved for the customer is worth the investment in terms of what they're going to get for that little extra bit of cost.

So how can you make this work for you? Go back to those 5-7 popular products and simply ask yourself: "Is there an upgraded and/or premium version of this that I can offer to my customers?"

There always is. And often times, you can make a premium version without hardly any additional hard cost, if you focus on intangibles. Let me give you an example...

Let's say you own a high-end restaurant. One premium version you can offer to your clients is the "immediate seating" club. For a small fee each year, these customers can guarantee that they get seated as soon as they enter the restaurant. In this case, you're selling time and convenience, not a product. That has a lot of value in this day and age.

Or you could even create a special area for preferred customers that has a much more luxurious feel to it, to make them enjoy the atmosphere more. Again, you're selling luxury, not a product... another intangible.

The final sales technique you should consider using is "Packaged Selling". Most people prefer to have someone else make the decision for them, so they don't have any responsibility in the matter.

Let's return to the flooring example again... Why not create an "Active Lifestyle Package". This would be for people with young children, maybe pets as well, or for those who have high traffic homes.

For this special package, you choose the carpet, padding, vinyl and tile options, and then sell it as a package, instead of each component on its own.

This allows you to already INCLUDE the premium versions, or the products that have the highest profit margins.

Your customers are more likely to say Yes if you do it right, since it's now easier for them to say Yes. Then, the next logical step is to up-sell them to an even more deluxe package. You see! In this case it could be the "Active-but-Luxurious Lifestyle Package."

Let's go back to our restaurant example now... Let's design the "Romance Package". In this case, the customer would get a limo to pick them up at their door, they get a special table near the fireplace that is more secluded, they get a vase filled with beautiful flowers that they get to take home and keep (including the vase), and they get a special "Lover's Dessert" for the lucky couple to share.

You're no longer in the restaurant business... you're in the *romance business...* and you can charge *a lot more* for that!

At the very least, you need to create one "package" that you can offer to a certain portion of your clients.

Make it much higher priced and more luxurious than normal so that even if only a handful of customers say yes to it each year, you'll have made a pretty good extra bit of profits without doing hardly much extra.

Alternatively, if you vehemently feel that high-end packages won't fare well in your type of industry (this is usually only the case when you're dealing with just tangible goods; that's why it's great to create packages with intangible items also), then at the very least for your high-end package, select items that all have relatively high margins, add up the total as if they were being purchased one at a time, then take 5-20% off the total price of the new package, and advertise that as the package price.

If you must go this route and provide a price-break in order to gain a customer (which is always my least recommended approach and in the long-run by far the most expensive), be sure not to take off any more than you have to. You don't need to reduce the price by very much (if any) for it to feel like a compelling offer to your audience if they can clearly see that the advantages and the value outweigh the cost.

The amount of money someone is willing to pay you will be in direct proportion to the amount of value *they perceive* in your offer and the amount of confidence they have in your ability to get them results and deliver on your promise.

When you make the benefits of doing business with your company so clearly obvious to your prospects and customers, they should easily and quickly come to the conclusion that they: "would have to be totally incompetent and completely crazy to work with anyone else but you, no matter what the price is that you're charging".

Just remember that you don't actually need to lower your price if you're offering and delivering massive value. So instead of lowering your prices or giving a discount just to get a new customer, try adding more value, ideally in the form of intangible items, to your offer in order to make it irresistible.

Remember about Pareto's Principle, also known as the Principle of Factor Sparsity, and of course most know it as the 80–20 rule... I want you to always keep it at the forefront of your mind when you are operating your business, so I'm going to repeat it for your benefit – it states that roughly *80% of the effects come from 20% of the causes*.

More applicably, it is overwhelmingly likely that 20% of your customers are bringing in 80% of your profits. But have you even identified who these top 20% most profitable customers of yours are yet?

However the real question is, are you doing enough to retain the long-term loyalty, and quite-frankly maximizing the profit-potential of your most profitable customers?

Mistake #3:
Not Understanding The Lifetime Value
Of A Customer

If you knew the potential lifetime value of even an average customer, you'd spend far more time making sure existing customers continued to use your services, and far less time trying to get new customers.

Let me give you an example: Let's say Lucy is 45 and spends $100 every week at her preferred grocery store. Lucy doesn't plan on moving any time soon, and has at least 15 more years of good shopping left in her.

So let's see, 15 years is 780 weeks. And at an average of $100 per week, that's $78,000. Now let's say you own that grocery store... Don't you think it would be prudent to come up with a strategy to *make sure* Lucy keeps coming back to you?

Now get this... A famous study done 20 years ago that was recently just re-tested and re-confirmed, found out what causes people to quit going to a store or a service provider. Here are the results:

9% - Leave because of competition...

Okay, so someone else might come along offering them a better deal, or better service. Or perhaps they have a location that's closer than yours. It sucks, but that is part of the game. Nonetheless the instructive thing to recognize is that you only lose 9% of your customers because of this.

9% - Leave because they move...

It's hard to get someone to come back to your store if they move halfway across the country. It's just the nature of the game (and I always refer to business as a game, because really, if you're not having fun in business, what's the point!). Anyway, some will move and won't ever return for reasons out of your control. So don't be overly concerned about these folks.

They probably (hopefully) did not move 'because of you'. If they did leave because of you, well, all I'm going to say, is that you can't create the solution to a problem with the same mind that created the problem. (*ie:* call me)

14% - Leave because of a complaint or dissatisfaction with service or product...

Okay, this can be worked on a bit, but one thing you must learn in business is you can't please everyone, nor do you want to. Anyway, although it's a fairly significant number and a big deal if any customers leave due to dissatisfaction, there is still something FAR, FAR greater and detrimental that causes your customers to go somewhere else.

It is greater than all these other factors combined. Here it is: **68% - Leave because of perceived apathy of the service provider...**

In other words, they feel you only look at them as a customer to get money from, and that you don't care about them. Notice the word 'perceived'.

You might very well care about them, but if you don't *show them* you care about them in a way that's unique and that isn't something that everyone else does, then there is no reason for them to remain loyal to you.

So if you don't have a specific ***customer-retention strategy*** in place, you're losing two-thirds or more of your previous customers! When you consider the potential lifetime value of a single customer, I don't know about you, but that would make most business owners sick to their stomach thinking about how much have been leaving on the table!

So what's the remedy? First, you need to increase the amount of communication you have with your past customers. At the very least, follow the "4 per day rule". Every business day, someone in your business should contact at least 4 past customers with a personal follow up, either by email, phone, direct-mail letter, or in person.

You should also consider a newsletter... and no, not those fancy, beautifully polished and "corporate looking" newsletters I'm sure you're familiar with. You need to take a more personal approach.

People don't fall in love with corporations. They fall in love with personalities. The first part of that word is "person". You have to open up to them. Let them know who you are and a little bit about what's going on in your life. You also have to show some character and a bit of humor, and style.

Think of why you're close friends with the friends you're close with. You should try to establish that same bond with your customers.

There are several strategies I use to do this. One of the best is with a monthly newsletter, which is something I'm great at crafting. If you're interested in getting some ideas for how to create these special customer-retention systems and/or newsletters, you can connect with me at **1-800-923-9495** or **Yes@CEO-HQ.com**.

Finally, someone who cares about you looks out for your best interest with no ulterior motive in mind. Again, that's where a newsletter comes in handy. Each month, you can create an article giving them tips on how to better their life, improve the value they can get from your services, and just things that can make them feel better about themselves.

And they're getting all this stuff just because they're a customer of yours! *That's* how you make someone feel special.

At any rate, you need to create some kind of customer retention campaign, and it doesn't always have to be a newsletter. Often it's all about just staying in contact with past customers, even just once every few months to let them know you're still thinking about them.

Now, although the next several strategies are typically only used (poorly) to focus on just getting new customers, patients and clients, they are still extremely effective and applicable (and extremely rarely ever used) for leveraging the two most profitable profit-growing activities of getting current customers to spend more and getting them to buy more often. But if you do need to focus on getting new customers, make sure you stick to the following five proven strategies...

The Top 5 Proven Strategies Using The Internet To Explode Your Sales Revenue

Explosive Strategy #1: Video Marketing

Would you believe that there are over 4 BILLION videos viewed per DAY (that's more than 120 BILLION videos viewed every month), and surprisingly that 70% of YouTube visitors come from outside the US? What's more, YouTube is the #2 search engine on the net internet!

Yes you did read that correctly – no it is not a typo. At the time of writing this book (and at first printing), YouTube has now been for a few years, the #2 most popular search engine on the internet, which means that right now somebody is likely searching for your services (or services similar to yours) online in the form of a video.

How-to videos are a really great way to market your brand on YouTube without having people put up their defenses from an obvious, blatant sales video. It's in our nature to learn and improve; staying engaged with your audience through a short web-based video every now and then endears them to your company and brand.

That's the power of video marketing. You can totally dominate your market with it. Let me show you how this is possible on a much smaller budget than would be required to run infomercials 24/7, and yet have the same effect, AND be able to engender more trust and respect with your customers than ever before!

Explosive Strategy #2: Social Media Marketing

Social Media is all the rage right now. With over 850,000,000 members on Facebook alone, Social Media Marketing is a giant that cannot be ignored. Social networks have changed the way people research and make buying decisions. When leveraged in your favour you'll have the opportunity to build more trust, respect, and credibility than ever before.

Social media can be a great resource for increasing sales, generating leads, and help with inbound marketing. But it doesn't always work for all businesses, because most businesses don't know how to use it properly.

Not only do you have to tailor your message to the audience that you're promoting to, but you actually need to have a strategic plan of implementation.

Imagine being able to have feedback on how to improve your business, and sell more on a daily basis. Imagine being able to turn every customer into a potential raving fan who will advertise for you. I can make it happen, and you can secure my services exclusively in your local market. Just contact me before your competition does. If you're reading this, then that means likely they are too. And as I mentioned previously, you can secure my services exclusively in your local market. In other words, I will work with only one business in your industry in your geographic area.

Explosive Strategy #3: Capture Leads & Follow-Up

To capture leads and get more people to buy from you, there's more you can do with your website than just making it look nice and presentable. For instance, the Law of Reciprocity in social psychology refers to responding to a positive action with another positive action. In other words, rewarding kind actions.

Use this human predisposition to capture more leads by offering valuable free incentives, such as exclusive discounts, coupons, consumer awareness reports, apps, software, audio, video or other downloadable content. In exchange, ask for their contact details, which you can use to follow-up with right away, as well as ethically use to continue to market to them long into the future for a tremendously high ROI (if done properly).

The more browsers you're able to attract — and more importantly, retain — in your marketing funnel, the more likely they will convert into actual buyers.

By investing in and implementing our automated client-acquisition-and-retention system, it will translate into greater sales, higher returns on investment and more time at hand for you to concentrate on improving your service delivery without having to worry about looking for new leads and new customers/clients/patients/cases.

You could attempt this strategy on your own if you have to, or you can call us to properly implement it all for you.

Explosive Strategy #4: Paying For Instant Visibility

Looking for instant traffic? Interested in targeting your potential customers with precisely targeted online ads where *you only pay when somebody clicks* on your ads? Get instant traffic online with a PPC marketing campaign!

So what exactly is PPC and why is it so compelling? Well, Pay-Per-Click (PPC) advertising, also known as Paid-Search, is a $34-Billion/year industry, bigger than Radio AND Cinema Advertising *combined,* and by 2016, it's expected to grow by 75% to $61.1-Billion per year!!

Did you know that you're losing out on gaining instant website visitors, potential leads and sales by not doing PPC? Did you know that PPC is the fastest way to drive instant traffic to your website? Without traffic, you are losing out on time, opportunities, customers and money to your competition.

Since it's the fastest way to drive instant traffic to your website, it's especially useful for direct-response campaigns where instant and direct action is the goal from target customers. This scenario also allows for the cost-per-click to be measured immediately against conversions or sales to determine and optimize the ROI.

So why choose Consulting Experts Online for your PPC? Choosing us will liberate you from learning the highly technical skills required to run a PPC campaign successfully. You can focus on building and running your business while we do the job of increasing your quality leads and customers through PPC. We take the time to understand your business, your objectives, your product or service, your target market and their online behavior for us to deliver PPC results of the highest performance.

Explosive Strategy #5: Local Search Visibility

Did you know that about 86% of consumers start their search online, and that about 82% of all searches done on Google include a local component or search-term modifier (like "Metrotown Roofing Contractors")?

This means that every search for every term will have only the local companies showing up that have figured out how to become visible at the top of all the major search engines by getting listed in all of the online local directories.

Optimizing your website to show up at the top of the search engines, otherwise known as Search Engine Optimization (or SEO), is a key component of getting found by your potential customers. SEO is both an art and a science, and a constantly changing ever-evolving one at that, and is a key ingredient for you to get new customers from the internet.

It goes without saying that your customers can't hire you or buy from you if they can't find you online.

I make sure that your local business IS found on Google and everywhere else... for all the keywords and search-terms that you need to rank for, so that everyone from your neighbors, friends, and family – to even your prospective customers or clients(!) can finally find YOU online – instead of your competitors, like they are now.

If you think that I just shared with you some pretty powerful marketing strategies in the first six chapters, well you may be surprised, but that's not even where my specialty in marketing is. Did you notice that none of those non-suck marketing secrets I shared with you had anything to do with the internet? But guess what, *that* is what I specialize in: High-ROI Online Marketing.

If all those high-R.O.I., totally non-suck strategies so far had nothing to do with the internet, just imagine the impact it'll have on your business if you qualify to plug into my company's non-suck online marketing systems.

Contact my office right now to have me and my team of Profit-Boosting Marketing Experts get your website to show up in the local Google maps listings, guaranteed.

I don't say it to brag or boast, I say it because it is true: My team is so damn kick-ass good at what they do that we can ethically guarantee you top spots in Google.

Do NOT wait. This is not a false-scarcity marketing tactic here. I will only work with just ONE company in the same category or industry exclusively for each city.

I must emphasize this here, because if any one of your competitors who is in the same industry-and-region as you gets a hold of this book -(let me be clear, they most certainly probably will; marketing is what my company is kinda-sorta good at just a little bit, after all)- and they call me first, ready to take their business to the next level –before you're ready to– I do sincerely apologize but I simply won't be willing to work with you in the future when you are ready if your competitor has already applied before you. My clients tend to stick around with us for years, so we're talking many years, if ever, before another opportunity for you to become a client of ours becomes available again.

So if the timing is right for you right now, and you feel we might be able to help take your business to the next level, apply now if this resonates with you. If this does resonate with you, there's a reason for it... Carpe Diem!

www.CEO-HQ.com/activateprofits

About The Author

Author, speaker, business-development consultant, and profit-boosting marketing engineer, Jayson "the profit-doctor" Peppar is an expert at helping small businesses and medium-size enterprises gain a dominant position over their competition and dominate their marketplace.

Jayson specializes in helping local and national entrepreneurs, business owners, marketing directors and special-event coordinators to gain a competitive advantage in their local or national marketplace, both on the internet and offline. He makes sure that his hand-selected clients are able to be "found" on the internet, ensures they always have a full pipeline of high-quality leads, and helps them to convert these potential clients of theirs (and even the old, stale, cold clients of theirs) into loyal lifetime fans and advocates.

Explosive business growth, no matter what industry you are in, does not happen by accident...

Jayson and his team at Consulting Experts Online engineer and implement proven marketing systems that help you leverage the three keys to explosive growth and massively increase profits in your business.

If you are serious about leveraging these proven high-R.O.I. marketing systems to dramatically improve your own company's bottom line, and would like to schedule a no-obligation marketing assessment and competitive analysis diagnostic consultation (valued at $1,495 at no cost to you) to see if you qualify to have The Profit-Doctor and his team engineer a comprehensive High-ROI Non-Suck Marketing Blueprint for your company, go to

www.NonSuckMarketingBook.com/apply

A Few Testimonials

Here is what just some of Jayson's clients have to say about the results he and his agency are able to create for their businesses:

"Consulting Experts Online is heads-and-shoulders above other SEO companies. After disappointing results from a number of SEO resources, I was fortunate to engage the services of Jayson's company.

Consulting Experts Online goes far beyond SEO and supports business development with creative ideas, suggestions of resources, and an ability to "see the big picture" of increasing not just sales and revenue, but also more importantly of increasing actual PROFITS.

A client of Jayson Peppar and Consulting Experts Online benefits from SEO excellence combined with keen marketing insights. I appreciate all of their excellent services and I give them my highest recommendation."

~ Charles Carracedo, CFP
Associate Financial Planner, Stoker Ostler
Scottsdale, Arizona

"Jayson is dedicated to providing great service and has always achieved really great results for our team.

His experience and expertise in marketing and the systems he has applied to our business have increased our sales by over 230% over the last several months.

He has boundless energy and the ability to work with diverse opinions and styles in order to maximize profitability. Jayson is constantly adding value to our business whether it's suggesting/implementing another creative way to market our services, or going above and beyond the scope-of-work service contract with his occasional observations and recommendations of what we should or shouldn't be doing, even if it doesn't have to do with marketing per-se. Working with J.P. and C.E.O. is always a great experience and we're really glad he was recommended to us and we highly recommend him to help your business become more successful as well."

~ Alexandra Romanov
Partner at Rant Finance Network
Greater St. Louis Area, Missouri

"I've had the pleasure of doing business with Jayson Peppar over the past few years, and he and his team continues to impress the heck out of me with their knowledge in SEO, search engine marketing, blogging, and not to mention with their dedication to excellent service. Jayson is very dependable and has high integrity; anyone would benefit by employing the services of Jayson Peppar and Consulting Experts Online. We have worked on many projects together and I'm looking forward to our continued business relationship."

~ John Knoewles
Marketing Manager, CMS Customer Solutions
San Antonio, Texas

"What more can I say? - Jayson Peppar delivered better than expected results. He is one of those rare professionals who can focus on the details and can also have far sighted strategic visions and ideas with strong leadership. Jayson is a reliable, proactive professional and delivers results. Jayson is a skilled business person and marketer that is able to take a concept to reality.

He is a dedicated professional to his work and to the people to whom he is offering high quality services. Jayson and his services is just what my company needed to get back on track. He has my full vote of confidence - I recommend him and his company if you want your company to grow...

As an ongoing investment that continues to reap me increasingly profitable results, I look forward to working with Jayson Peppar and his team long into the future..."

~ David Diaz
Owner, Diaz Technology Services
Peabody, Massachusetts

"Jayson is dedicated to helping you and your business take a quantum leap toward your goals. I highly recommend Jayson and his services."

~ Mark Johnson
Professional Trainer & Life Coach
Managing Partner, Success Innovations Inc.
Owner, Mark Johnson Consulting
Didsbury, Alberta

> "He's one of the best marketing professionals I have had the privilege to meet and work with. He not only brings a lot of online marketing expertise, but also certainly knows how to turn to advertising from a cost center to a profit center. A true leader in this space and highly-skilled expert who gets very profitable results!"

~ Alex Stevenson
Vice President, Trinetics
Denver, Colorado

> "Awesome Choice! I originally got in touch with Jayson to help us modernize our church's website and make it more up to date looking and more dynamic.
>
> It was the best call I could have made. Prior to Jayson, I contacted two other web design companies but never really got off the ground with them.
>
> After my first discussion with JP, I knew this was the right guy for the job. He's not looking to pigeonhole you into any templates or pre-configured designs. He finds out your needs and gives you options on the best way to accomplish the task. He incorporates all your ideas, suggestions, etc, so you're in control of the design while he and his team of Experts does all the heavy lifting. During the design I was frequently sent updates and kept in the loop as the job progressed.
>
> Our church was so pleased with the results that I recommended him to my boss and had him design a site for our company and he also developed a strategic marketing plan to help our company get more clients and contracts by doing "SEO" and "PPC". I'm not sure of all the exact details, but I know for

sure my boss is a lot more profitable now because he came up to me in private last month completely out of the blue and gave me a very large bonus check and told me to not tell anyone else about it!!

Whether you're looking for a simple 2-3 page website or an elaborate site that involves heavy coding and custom coded scripts and all that, and even a website marketing plan and implementation too, I'll encourage anyone to call him... you'll be very pleased."

~ Clinton Rushing
West Houston Church
Good Home Inspection
Houston, Texas

Notes

_____

_____

_____

_____

_____

_____

_____

_____

_____

_____

_____

_____

_____

_____

_____

_____

Notes

_____

_____

_____

_____

_____

_____

_____

_____

_____

_____

_____

_____

_____

_____

_____

Notes

_____

_____

_____

_____

_____

_____

_____

_____

_____

_____

_____

_____

_____

_____

_____

Notes

_____

_____

_____

_____

_____

_____

_____

_____

_____

_____

_____

_____

_____

_____

_____

_____

$1,495.00 value

COMPETITIVE ANALYSIS & MARKETING ASSESSMENT DIAGNOSTIC CONSULTATION

This offer is part of a limited marketing test and will be revoked at any time without notice. Don't miss out, claim right now.

___ **Yes!** I want to schedule a private consultation with you to discuss hiring you as my marketing consultant. I understand your services are in high-demand and your time is limited. I understand that you will only work with just one industry per area, and that there's a very real possibility I may not even qualify to hire you. That's why I'm acting now to take advantage of this gift certificate (a $1,495 value) and am requesting to schedule a private Competitive Analysis & Marketing Assessment Diagnostic Consultation with you at your next available appointment.

During my Business Diagnostic Consultation you will give me a complete marketing assessment, and then share exactly what I need to get more profitable online:

- Information that is *specific to me*, from a qualified business growth expert.

- Finally! *Actionable advice* on how I can grow my business quickly.

- The potential opportunity to work with you as your client and possibly double my business over the coming year. If there's availability, I understand you are one of the premiere profit-boosting high-ROI marketing experts to small businesses, and that demand for your services is exponentially increasing!

I'm sick of wasting my time and money on false solutions and promises that don't deliver. I'm ready to commit 100% to do whatever it takes to achieve my goals and take action now.

Furthermore, I understand that if I qualify to hire you as my marketing consultant, I'm not only going to reactivate past customers and get new customers in minimal time, but I'm also going to build a solid foundation to ensure I continue to grow my business.

For these reasons, I am contacting your office right away to claim this gift certificate and schedule my complimentary $1,495 Competitive Analysis & Marketing Assessment Diagnostic Consultation, at no cost and no obligation to me.

`[This offer is part of a limited marketing test and it WILL be revoked after 1000 copies of this book have been sold. Don't miss out, claim right now!]`

www.NonSuckMarketingBook.com/activateprofits